An Easy Learning Guide

FRENCH

Skill Builders For Beginners

Nilusha Judha

First Published in December 2021

ISBN: 978-93-5472-790-0

BLUEROSE PUBLISHERS

www.bluerosepublishers.com

info@bluerosepublishers.com

+91 8882 898 898

Cover Design:

Geetika

Typographic Design:

Namrata Saini

Distributed by: BlueRose, Amazon, Flipkart, Shopclues

La table des matières
(Table of Contents)

About the Author

Bonjour,

Je m'appelle Nilusha Judha.

I was born in Democratic Republic of Congo, brought up and studied in Zambia and South Africa. I completed my Masters in India.

As I love teaching children, I decided to teach French from the age group of three years and above. Learning French helps one to express themselves and gain self-confidence as French is a very creative and a beautiful language.

So, I went ahead and formed my brand. "I Know You Know Français". And, today you are reading a book by me, which will help anyone to master the essentials of French vocabulary through focused practice.

This book is very colourful and in an inviting format, it is very easy-to-follow, it will help to build ones confidence and make French learning more enjoyable. This book will also help to keep one engaged with activities and motivate them to learn French further.

Bonne Chance,

Nilusha Judha

Le Français dans le monde

(French throughout the world)

Did you know that people throughout the world speak French and have for many years?

Today, French is an official language in twenty nine countries. French is Spoken in fifty three countries, making it one of the most - widespread languages of the world.

French is spoken as the official language in Belgium, Switzerland, Luxembourg, Congo, Canada, France, Mali and many more other countries.

French is also known as the most beautiful spoken language.

About forty five percent of modern English words are of French origin.

French is the second most widely learned language after English and the sixth widely spoken language.

Les alphabets
(The Alphabet)

Aa		l'ananas
Bb	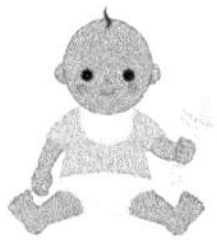	le bébé
Cc		le chat
Dd	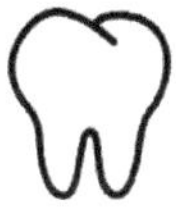	la dent
Ee		l'éléphant
Ff		la fenêtre

Gg	 Journal	la guitare
Hh		la hache
Ii		l’insecte
Jj		le journal
Kk		le koala
Ll		la lampe
Mm		la maison

Nn		la neige
Oo		l'océan
Pp		le pain
Qq		La quille
Rr		la règle
Ss		la scie
Tt		la table
Uu		l'usine

Vv		la voiture
Ww		le wagon
Xx		le xylophone
Yy		les yeux
Zz		le zèbre

Les salutations
(Greetings)

Bonjour - Good morning

Bon après-midi - Good afternoon

Bonsoir - Good evening

Bonne nuit - Good night

Salut - Hi

Au revoir - Goodbye

Merci - Thank you

De rien - Welcome

Bienvenue - Welcome (home)

Désolé - Sorry

S'il vous plaît - Please

Comment t'appelles-tu? - What's your name?

Je m'appelle - My name is

Joyeux / Bon anniversaire - Happy birthday

Joyeux anniversaire - Happy anniversary

Joyeux Noël - Merry Christmas

Bonnes fêtes - Happy holidays

Bonne année - Happy new year

Félicitations - Congratulations

Rétablis- toi vite - Get well soon

Bon appétit - Have a good meal

Bon voyage - Happy journey

Bonnes vacances - Happy holidays

Bonne chance - Good luck

Santé! - Cheers

Bonne soirée - Have a good evening

Bonne journée - Have a good day

Enchanté - Nice to meet you

Coucou - Hi

Quoi de neuf? - What's up?

Tout sur moi
(All about me)

Bonjour,

Je m'appelle - My name is

J'ai ___ ans - I am ___ years old

Je suis indien(ne) - I am Indian

J'habite à Mumbai - I live in Mumbai

Je suis étudiant(e) - I am a student

J'étudie à - I study at

Mes meilleur(e)s ami(e)s s'appellent - My best friends are

Ma couleur préférée est - My favourite colour is

Jai les cheveux longs - I have long hair

J'ai les cheveux noirs - I have black hair

J'ai les yeux bruns - I have brown eyes

J'aime le chocolat - I love chocolates

Activity

Tout sur moi

Draw a picture of yourself

Q. Fill in the blanks

1. Je m'appelle _______________.
2. J'ai _______ans.
3. J'habite à __________________.
4. Je vais à l'école __________________.
5. Je suis _________________________.

Les nombres
(Numbers)

1	un	
2	deux	
3	trois	
4	quatre	
5	cinq	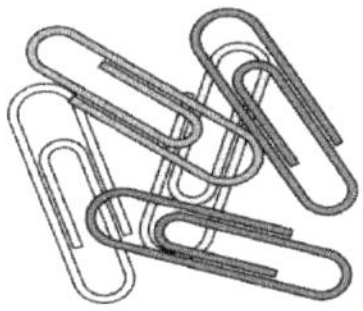

6	**six**	
7	**sept**	
8	**huit**	
9	**neuf**	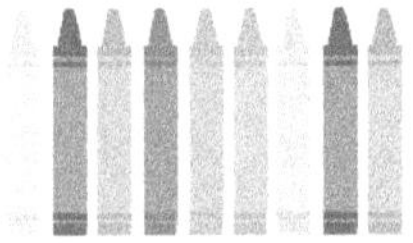
10	**dix**	

11	**onze**	
12	**douze**	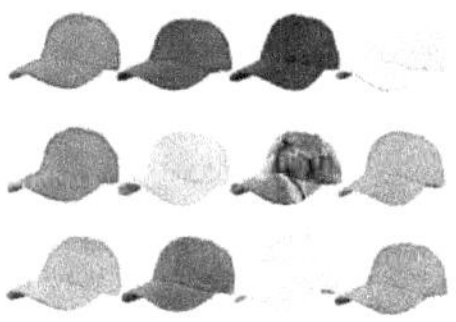
13	**treize**	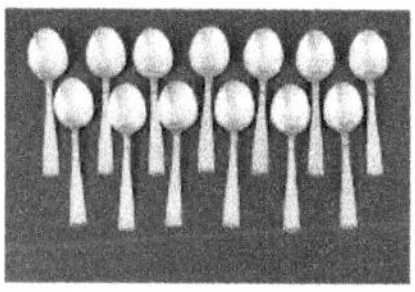
14	**quatorze**	
15	**quinze**	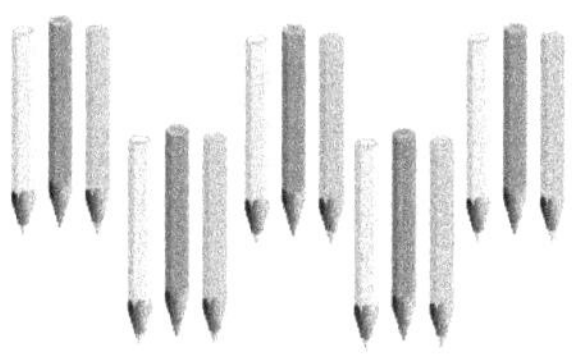

16	seize	
17	dix-sept	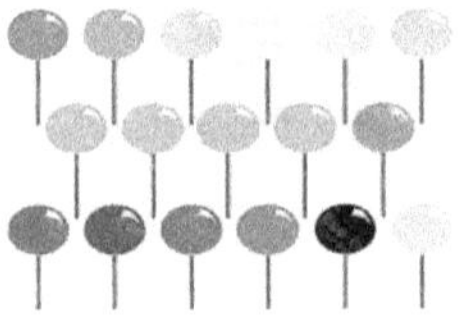
18	dix-huit	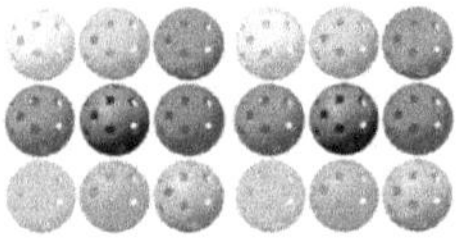
19	dix-neuf	
20	vingt	

Les nombres

1 un	2 deux	3 trois	4 quatre	5 cinq	6 six	7 sept	8 huit	9 neuf	10 dix
11 onze	12 douze	13 treize	14 quatorze	15 quinze	16 seize	17 dix-sept	18 dix-huit	19 dix-neuf	20 vingt
21 vingt et un	22 vingt-deux	23 vingt-trois	24 vingt-quatre	25 vingt-cinq	26 vingt-six	27 vingt-sept	28 vingt-huit	29 vingt-neuf	30 trente
31 trente et un	32 trente-deux	33 trente-trois	34 trente-quatre	35 trente-cinq	36 trente-six	37 trente-sept	38 trente-huit	39 trente-neuf	40 quarante
41 quarante et un	42 quarante-deux	43 quarante-trois	44 quarante-quatre	45 quarante-cinq	46 quarante-six	47 quarante-sept	48 quarante-huit	49 quarante-neuf	50 cinquante
51 cinquante et un	52 cinquante-deux	53 cinquante-trois	54 cinquante-quatre	55 cinquante-cinq	56 cinquante-six	57 cinquante-sept	58 cinquante-huit	59 cinquante-neuf	60 soixante
61 soixante et un	62 soixante-deux	63 soixante-trois	64 soixante-quatre	65 soixante-cinq	66 soixante-six	67 soixante-sept	68 soixante-huit	69 soixante-neuf	70 soixante-dix
71 soixante et onze	72 soixante-douze	73 soixante-treize	74 soixante-quatorze	75 soixante-quinze	76 soixante-seize	77 soixante-dix- sept	78 soixante-dix- huit	79 soixante-dix- neuf	80 quatre-vingts
81 quatre-vingt- un	82 quatre-vingt- deux	83 quatre-vingt- trois	84 quatre-vingt-quatre	85 quatre-vingt- cinq	86 quatre-vingt- six	87 quatre-vingt- sept	88 quatre-vingt- huit	89 quatre-vingt- neuf	90 quatre-vingt-dix
91 quatre-vingt- onze	92 quatre-vingt- douze	93 quatre-vingt- treize	94 quatre-vingt-quatorze	95 quatre-vingt-quinze	96 quatre-vingt- seize	97 quatre-vingt- dix-sept	98 quatre-vingt- dix-huit	99 quatre-vingt- dix-neuf	100 cent

Activity

Q1. Match the numbers to the corresponding boxes

SIX	SEPT	HUIT
☐	☐	☐

NEUF	DIX	
☐	☐	6 7 8 9 10

Activity

Q2. Match the number of things on the left to the number and match the word spelling on the right to the numbers in the middle

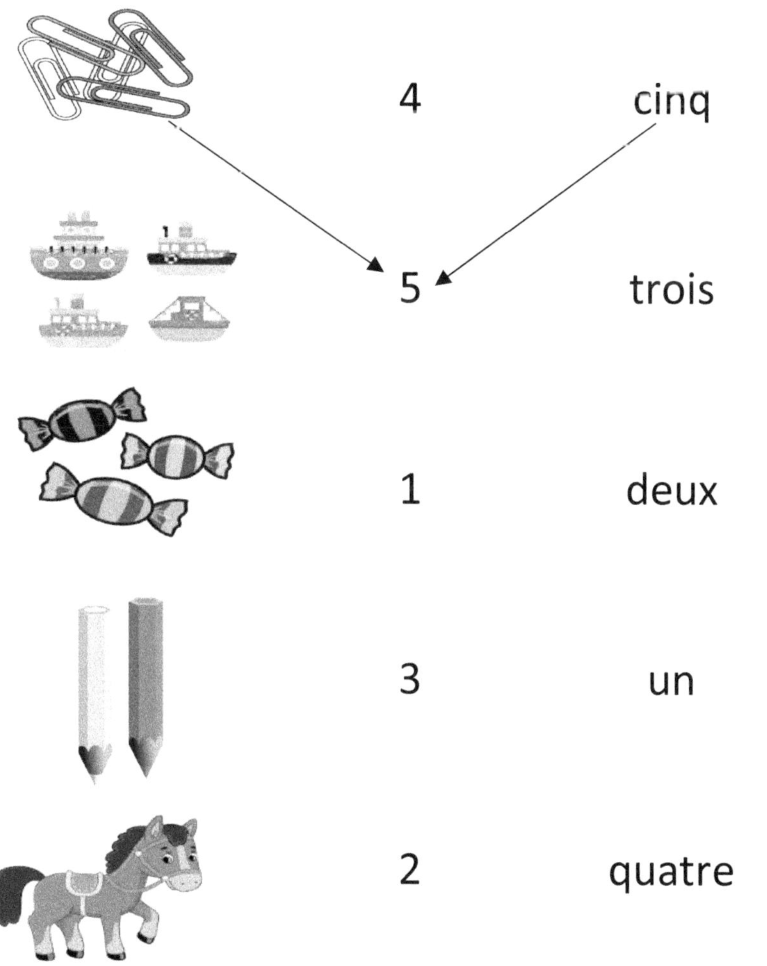

Quelle heure est-il?
(What time is it?)

Quelle heure est-il? (What time is it?)

À quelle heure? (At what time?)

Il est..... heures (It is __ o'clock)

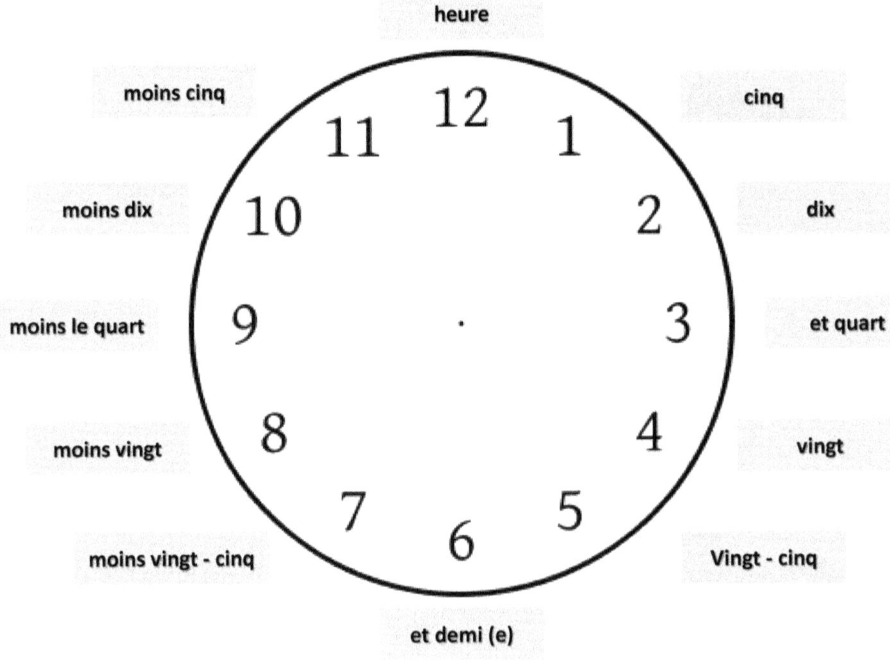

✓ Terms to remember:

- du matin - in the morning
- du soir - in the evening
- de l'après-midi - in the afternoon
- et quart - quarter past
- moins le quart - quarter to
- et demie - half past
- presque - nearly
- environ - about/ roughly
- minuit - midnight
- midi - midday

There are two ways of telling time in French:

1. Il est dix heures du matin = 10.00 a.m.
   Il est dix heures du soir = 10.00 p.m.
   Il est une heure de l'après-midi = 1.00 p.m.
   Il est une heure de la nuit = 1.00 a.m.

2. Il est 14h00 = 14 hours, commonly used for train or air time tables. This form is increasingly popular in day-to-day life as well. The 24hr clock.

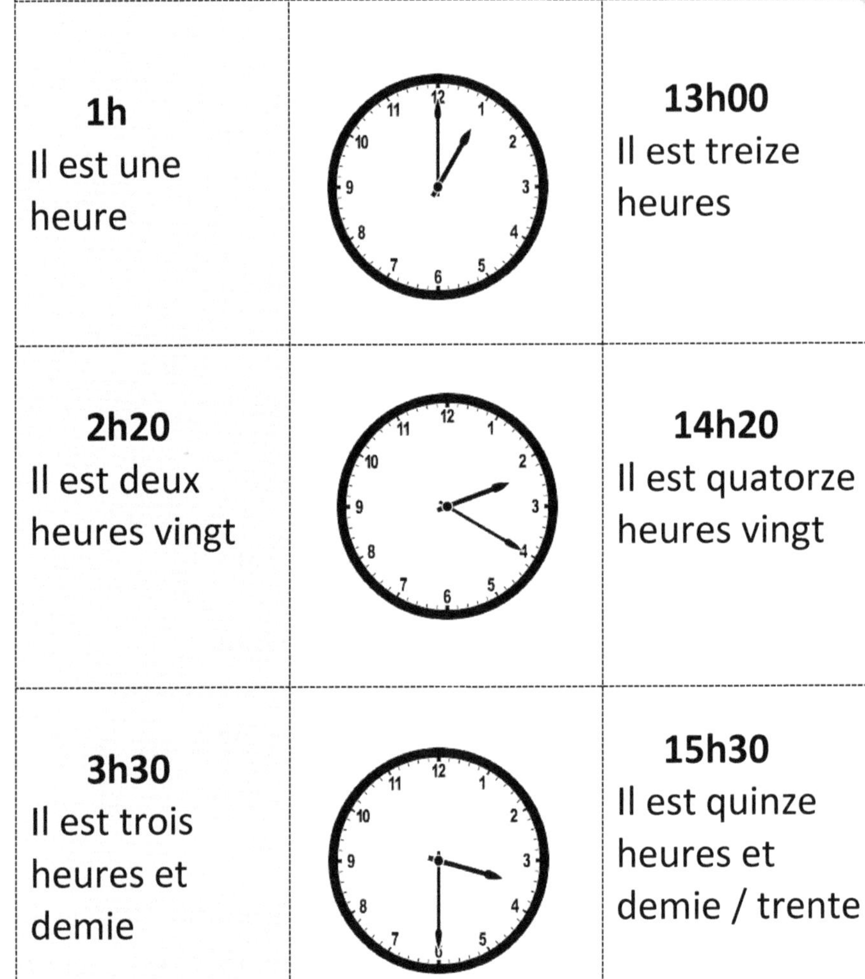

1h Il est une heure		**13h00** Il est treize heures
2h20 Il est deux heures vingt		**14h20** Il est quatorze heures vingt
3h30 Il est trois heures et demie		**15h30** Il est quinze heures et demie / trente

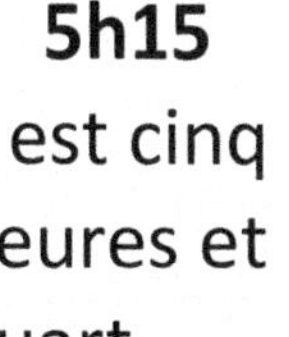 **5h15** Il est cinq heures et quart		**17h15** Il est dix-sept heures quinze
7h45 Il est huit heures moins le quart		**19h45** Il est dix- neuf heures quarante -cinq
12h Il est midi		**00h** Il est minuit

Activity

Q. Draw the time in the boxes below

Il est 9h 05

Il est 3h

Il est 11h 25

Il est 4h 30

Il est 8h 45

Il est midi

Les couleurs
(Colours)

rouge/rouge	jaune/jaune	bleu/bleue
vert/verte	orange/orange	rose/rose
gris/grise	violet/violette	blanc/blanche
noir/noire	marron/marron	brun /brune

Points to remember:

- Each colour is written twice and the second colour is feminine.
- Sometimes the masculine and feminine colours are the same.
- You need to add an " s " to make the colours plural.
- Marron and Orange never change even in plural.
- Marron, Orange, Jaune, Rouge, Rose will never change; they will remain the same for both Masculine and Feminine.

Activity

Q1. Colour the pictures with the mentioned colours

orange	bleue
marron	
rose	rouge

Activity

Q2. Colour the rainbow below

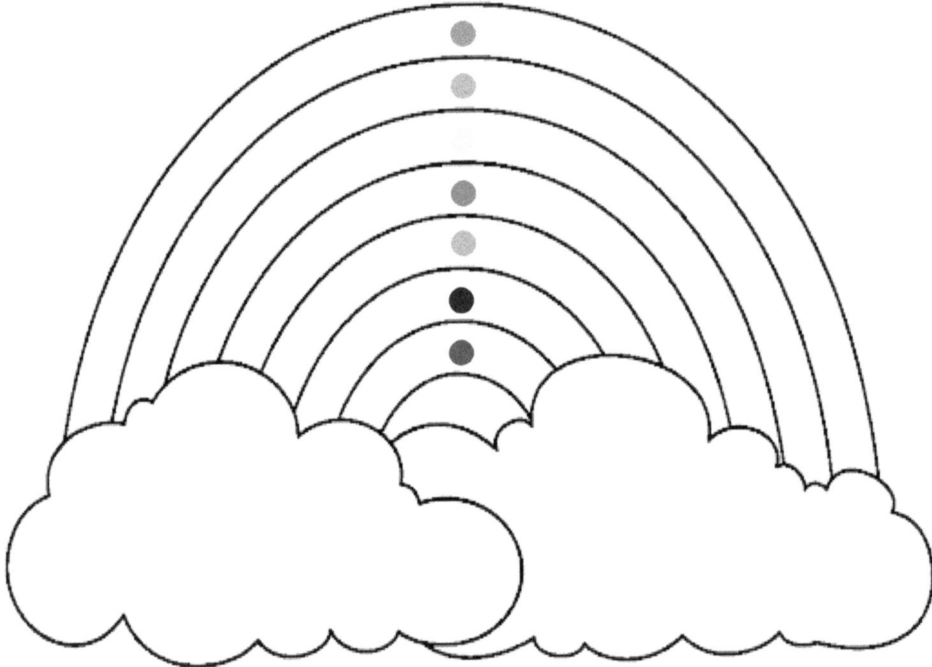

- ROUGE
- ORANGE
- JAUNE
- VERT
- BLEU
- INDIGO
- VIOLET

Les formes
(Shapes)

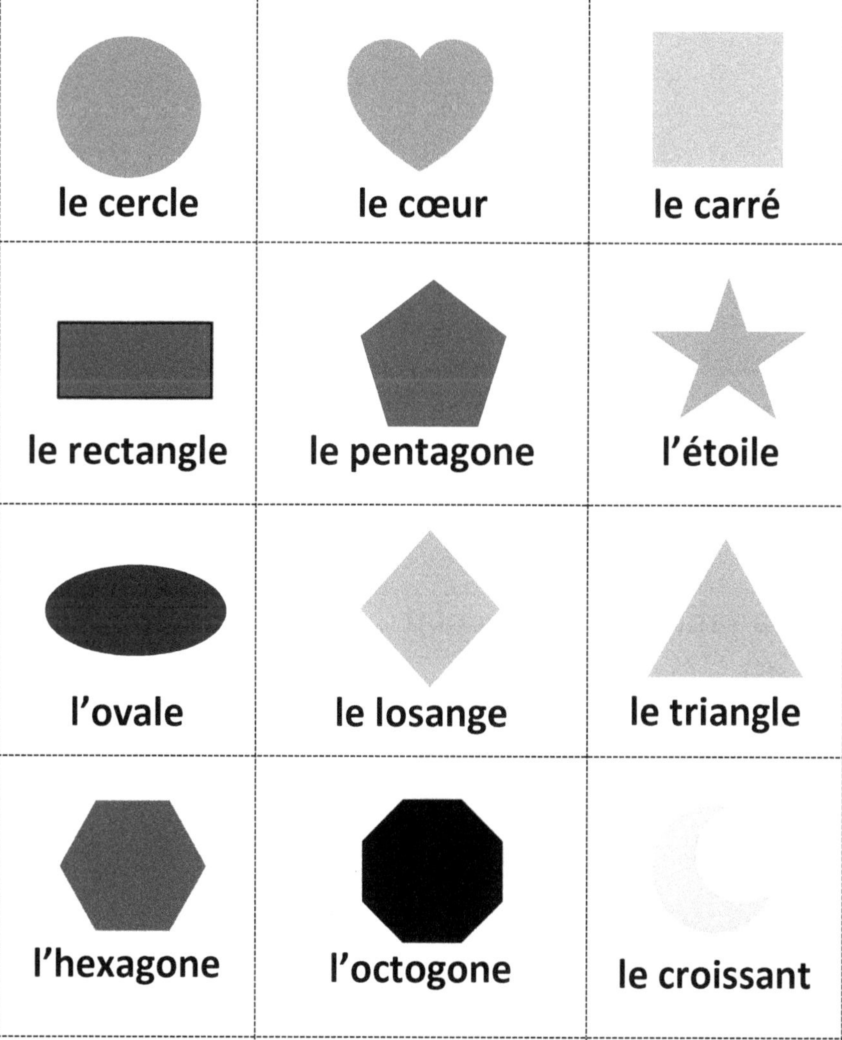

Activity

Q. Fill in the blanks with the appropriate words from the word bank below

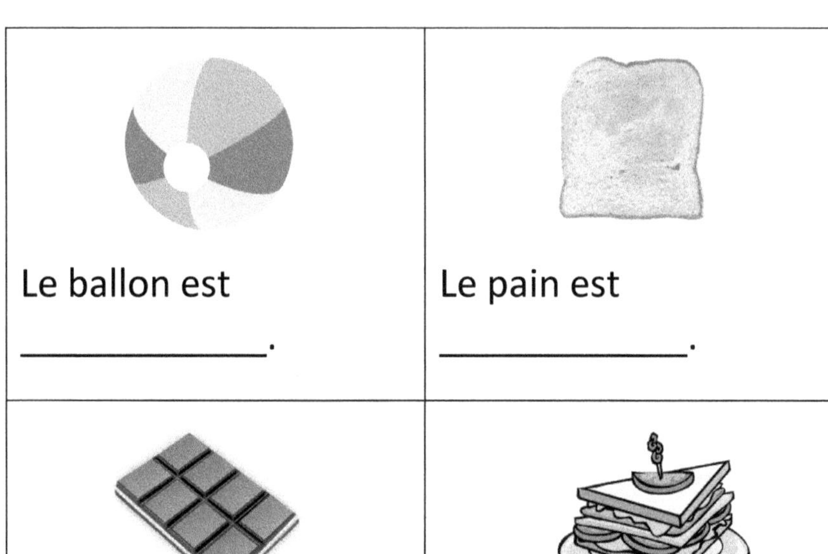

Le ballon est ______________.	Le pain est ______________.
La tablette de chocolat est__________________.	 Le sandwich est ______________.

- rond
- rectangulaire
- triangulaire
- carré

Les Jours de la Semaine
(The Days of the Week)

lundi	-	Monday
mardi	-	Tuesday
mercredi	-	Wednesday
jeudi	-	Thursday
vendredi	-	Friday
samedi	-	Saturday
dimanche	-	Sunday

Activity

Q. Fill in the blanks

hier Yesterday	**aujourd'hui** Today	**demain** Tomorrow
	lundi	
	mercredi	
	mardi	
	samedi	
	dimanche	
	jeudi	

Les mois de l'année
(The Months of the Year)

janvier	-	January
février	-	February
mars	-	March
avril	-	April
mai	-	May
juin	-	June
juillet	-	July
août	-	August
septembre	-	September
octobre	-	October
novembre	-	November
décembre	-	December

Activity

Q. Write the months of the year in the correct order

1) ________________	novembre
2) ________________	août
3) ________________	juillet
4) ________________	mai
5) ________________	décembre
6) ________________	avril
7) ________________	octobre
8) ________________	mars
9) ________________	septembre
10) ________________	février
11) ________________	juin
12) ________________	Janvier

Les saisons
(The Seasons)

le printemps

l'été

l'automne

l'hiver

Le temps
(The Weather)

 la pluie	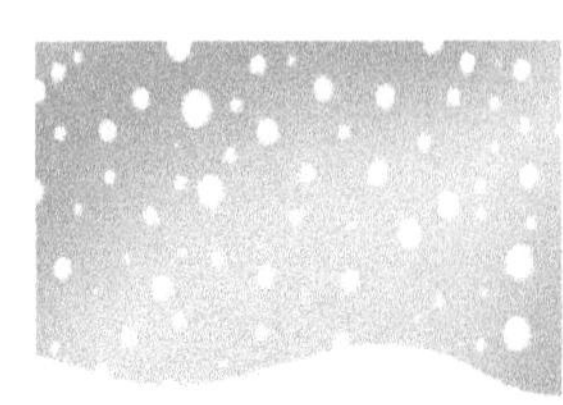 la neige
 le vent	 le soleil
 l'éclair	 le verglas

 les nuages	 le brouillard
 le tonnerre	 l'orage

Activity

Q.Identify the weather and draw it in the boxes below

<table>
<tr><td></td><td>Il y a du vent aujourd'hui.</td></tr>
<tr><td>Il y a des nuages aujourd'hui.</td><td>Il neige aujourd'hui.</td></tr>
<tr><td>Il pleut aujourd'hui.</td><td>Il fait beau aujourd'hui.</td></tr>
</table>

Les animaux
(Animals)

 le chien	 le chat	 la vache
 le cheval	 le cochon	 le mouton
 la fourmi	 le poisson	 le poisson rouge
 la tortue	 la souris	 le serpent

la mouche
le lion
le tigre
le loup
le zèbre
le singe
l'ours
les oiseaux
la grenouille
le crocodile
l'éléphant
la poule
la chèvre
le canard
l'agneau

Activity

Q. Look at the image and write the names of the animals

Les parties du corps
(Parts of the Body)

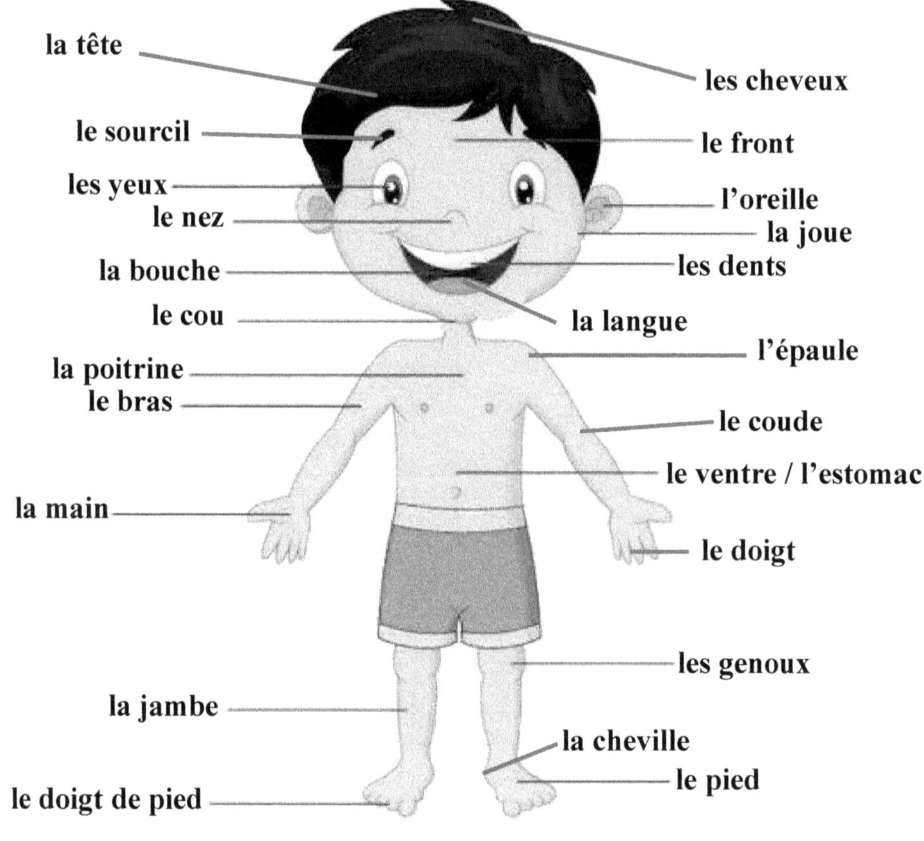

Activity

Q. Label the parts of the body

Les vêtements
(Clothing)

le manteau
le pull
le pyjama
les chaussures
les chaussettes
la veste
la casquette
l'imperméable
les sandales

Activity

Q. Label the clothing

Les sports
(Sports)

l'équitation

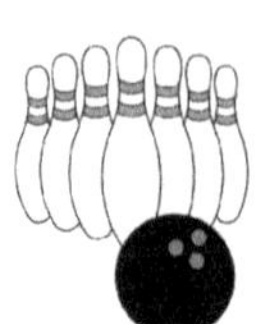

le bowling

la boxe

le karate

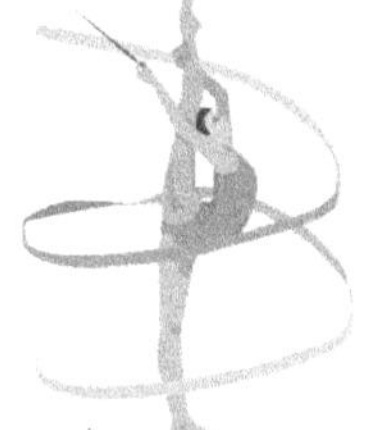

la gymnastique

le volley

le rugby

le judo

le badminton

Activity

Q. Fill in the blank

____

____

____

____

____

La famille
(The family)

1. **Le père** - the father
2. **La mère** - the mother
3. **Les parents** - the parents
4. **Le fils** - the son
5. **La fille** - the daughter
6. **Les enfants** - the kids
7. **Le grand- père** - the grandfather
8. **La grand- mère** - the grand mother
9. **Les grands- parents** - the grand parents
10. **L'oncle** - the uncle
11. **La tante** - the aunt
12. **Le cousin** - the cousin (m)
13. **La cousine** - the cousin (f)
14. **Le neveu** - the nephew
15. **La nièce** - the niece
16. **Le frère** - the brother
17. **La sœur** - the sister

Activity

Q. Draw the correct answer in the given boxes

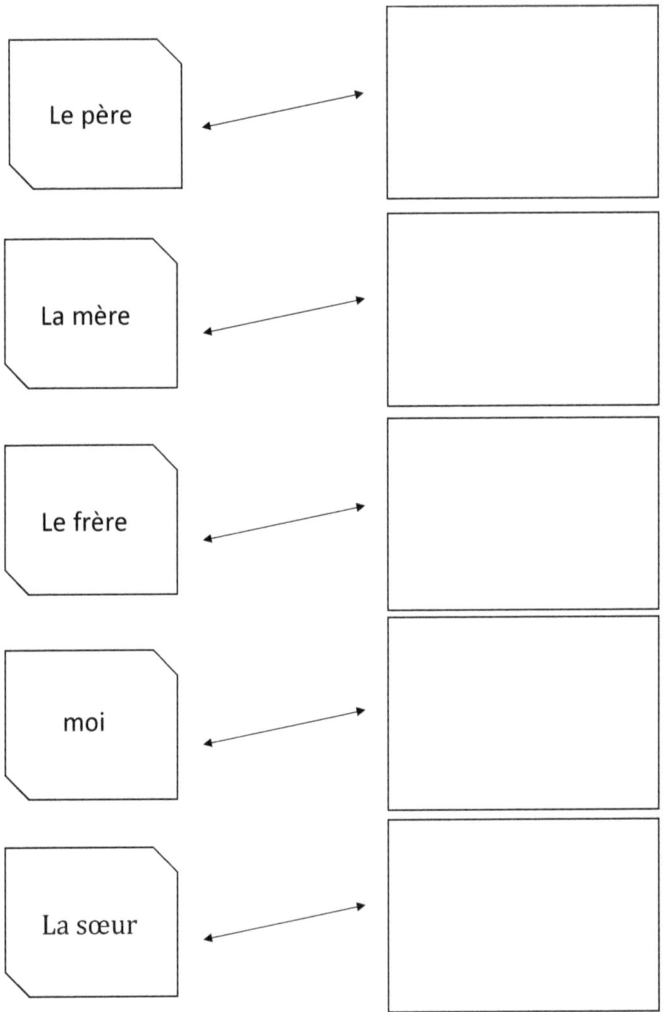

La maison
(The House)

 la chambre	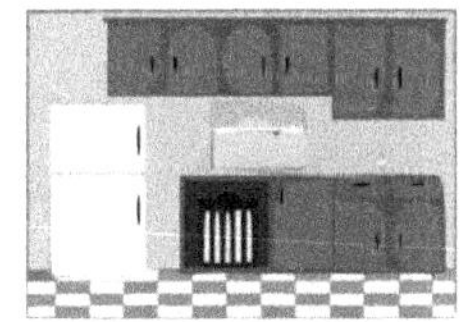 la cuisine	 le salon
 la salle à manger	 la salle de bains	 le toit
 le plancher	 le plafond	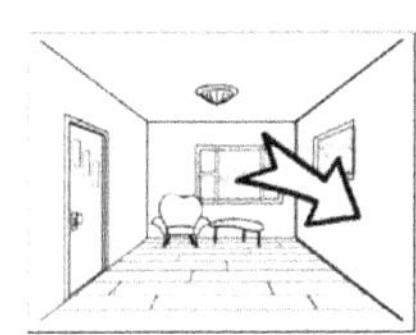 le mur

 la porte	 la fenêtre	 le placard
 l'escalier	 la cheminée	 le jardin

Les objets de la maison
(Objects in the House)

 la cuisinière	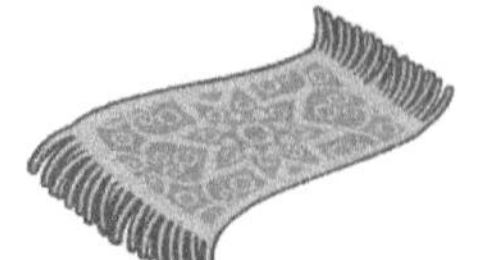 le tapis	 le téléphone
 la commode	 l'ordinateur	 la cheminée

Tu habites dans quelle sorte de maison?

(What kind of a house do you live in?)

 **dans une maison individuelle**	 **dans une ferme**
 **dans une maison jumelée**	 **dans un appartement**

Activity

Q. Label the parts of the house

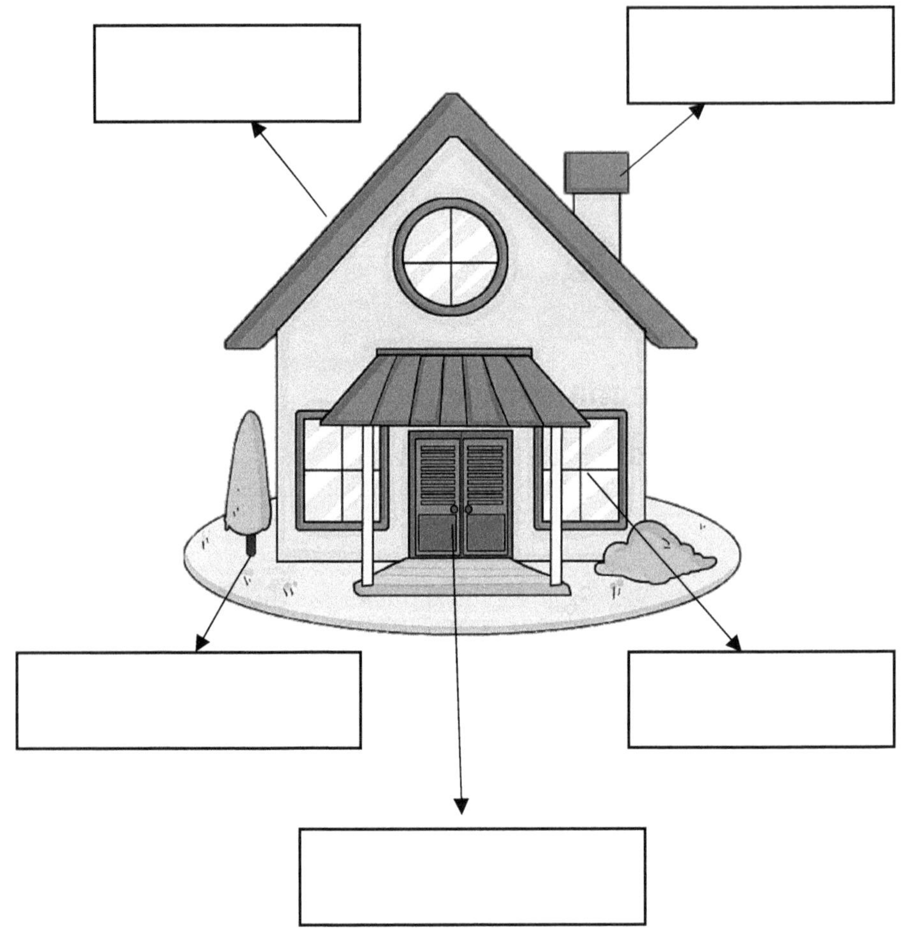

Activity

Q. Match the following

la chambre

le salon

la salle de bains

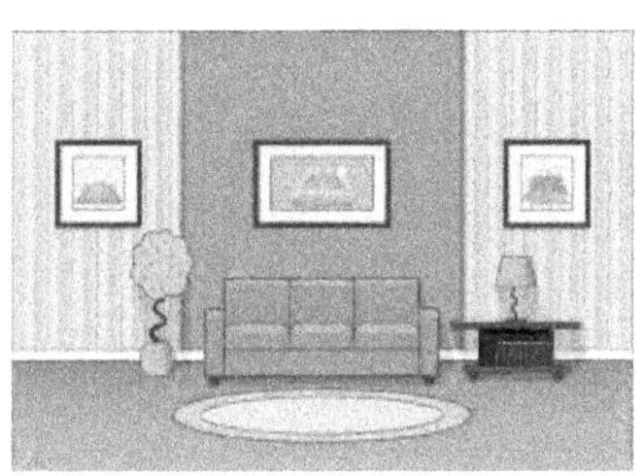

la cuisine

La nourriture
(Food)

1. **Le croissant** - the croissant
2. **Le café** - the coffee
3. **Le thé** - the tea
4. **Le pain** - the bread
5. **Le beurre** - the butter
6. **Les céréales** - the cereals
7. **Le jus de fruits** - the fruit juice
8. **Les œufs** - the eggs
9. **Le jambon** - the ham
10. **L'eau** - the water
11. **Le sandwich** - the sandwich
12. **Le riz** - the rice
13. **La salade** - the salad
14. **Le poisson** - the fish

15. **Le poulet** - the chicken
16. **La saucisse** - the sausages
17. **Les bonbons** - the sweets
18. **Les chocolats** - the chocolates
19. **Le gâteau** - the cake
20. **Les petits-gâteaux** - the cupcakes
21. **Le yaourt** - the yoghurt
22. **Le chocolat chaud** - the hot chocolate
23. **Le lait** - the milk
24. **La dinde** - the turkey
25. **L'omelette** - the omelette
26. **Les pâtes** - the pasta
27. **Les frites** - the fries
28. **Le fromage** - the cheese
29. **Le coca** - the coca cola
30. **Le bœuf** - the beef
31. **Le hamburger** - the burger

32. **La viande** - the meat
33. **Le sel** - the salt
34. **Le poivre** - the pepper
35. **Le sucre** - the sugar
36. **Le vin** - the wine
37. **La glace** - the ice cream
38. **La tarte** - the pie
39. **Les chips** - the crisps
40. **La sauce** - the sauce
41. **La pizza** - the pizza

Le petit déjeuner – breakfast

Le déjeuner – lunch

Le dîner – dinner

Activity

Q. Draw lines to match French food to the English word

le lait	cheese
le fromage	chicken
le poulet	milk
la glace	bread
le yaourt	ice cream
la pain	yoghurt
le chocolat	sausages
les pâtes	cake
le gâteau	pasta
la saucisse	chocolate

Les fruits
(Fruits)

la papaye
la pêche
la figue
le melon
les raisins
la poire
l'abricot
l'ananas
la framboise
le pample mousse
la pastèque
la grenade

Activity

Q. Write the names of the fruits

 ____________

 ____________

 ____________

 ____________

 ____________

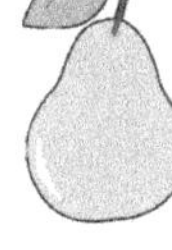 ____________

 ____________

 ____________

Les Légumes
(Vegetables)

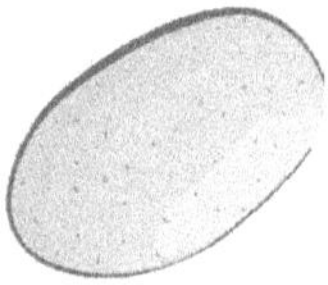 la pomme de terre	 le champignon	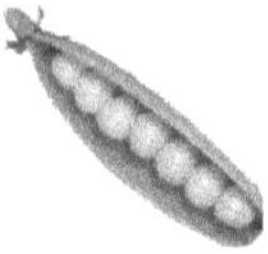 les petits pois
 les épinards	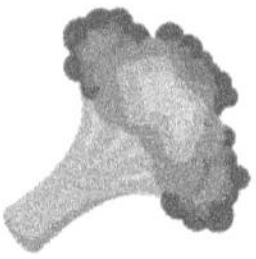 le brocoli	 le gombo
 la laitue	 le poivron	 le radis

l'oignon
le concombre
le chou
le maïs
les haricots verts
le chou-fleur
la courgette
l'aubergine
l'ail
la tomate
la carotte
la betterave

Activity

Q. Colour the vegetable basket below

À la table
(At the table)

1. le verre	6. la serviette
2. l'assiette	7. la nappe
3. la tasse	8. la fourchette
4. la soucoupe	9. le couteau
5. le bol	10. la cuillère

Les objets de la classe
(Objects in the Classroom)

1. **Le crayon** - the pencil
2. **Le stylo** - the pen
3. **La gomme** - the eraser
4. **Le taille - crayon** - the sharpener
5. **Le tableau** - the black board
6. **La trousse** - the pouch

7. **Le cartable** - the bag
8. **Le livre** - the text book
9. **Le cahier** - the notebook
10. **La feuille de papier** - the sheet of paper
11. **La craie** - the chalk
12. **La poubelle** - the dustbin
13. **Le banc** - the bench
14. **La chaise** - the chair
15. **La table** - the table
16. **L'ordinateur** - the computer
17. **La règle** - the ruler
18. **La carte** - the map
19. **Le dossier** - the document
20. **le dictionnaire** -the dictionary
21. **Le tableau noir** - the black board
22. **L'étagère** - the bookshelf
23. **Le placard** - the cupboard

Activity

Q. Identify the stationaries

____

____

____

____

____

____

Les professions
(Professions)

	Masculin	Féminin
Doctor	Médecin	Médecin
School teacher	Instituteur	Institutrice
Hairdresser	Coiffeur	Coiffeuse
Farmer	Fermier	Fermière
Architect	Architecte	Architecte
Lawyer	Avocat	Avocate
Writer	Écrivain	Écrivaine
Driver	Chauffeur	Chauffeuse
Actor	Acteur	Actrice

Director	Directeur	Directrice
Artist	Artiste	Artiste
Painter	Peintre	Peintre
Dentist	Dentiste	Dentiste
Carpenter	Charpentier	Charpentière
Postman/ woman	Facteur	Factrice
Nurse	Infirmier	Infirmière
Fire man/ woman	Pompier	Pompière
Scientist	Scientifique	Scientifique
Dancer	Danseur	Danseuse
Singer	Chanteur	Chanteuse
Astronaut	Astronaute	Astronaute

Electrician	Électricien	Électricienne
Waiter	Serveur	Serveuse
Engineer	Ingénieur	Ingénieure
Salesman/ Saleswoman	Vendeur	Vendeuse
Homemaker	Homme au foyer	Femme au foyer
Businessman/ woman	Homme d'affaires	Femme d'affaires
Accountant	Comptable	Comptable

Activity

Q. Write the names of the profession according to the picture

____

____

____

____

Les émotions
(Emotions)

Emotions	Masculin	Féminin
Happy	Heureux	Heureuse
Sad	Triste	Triste
Angry	Fâché	Fâchée
Bored	Ennuyé	Ennuyée
Delighted	Ravi	Ravie
Scared	Effrayé	Effrayée
Confused	Confus	Confuse
Tired	Fatigué	Fatiguée
Lazy	Paresseux	Paresseuse
Surprise	Surpris	Surprise
Grumpy	Grincheux	Grincheuse

Activity

Q. Draw the mentioned emotions in the circle

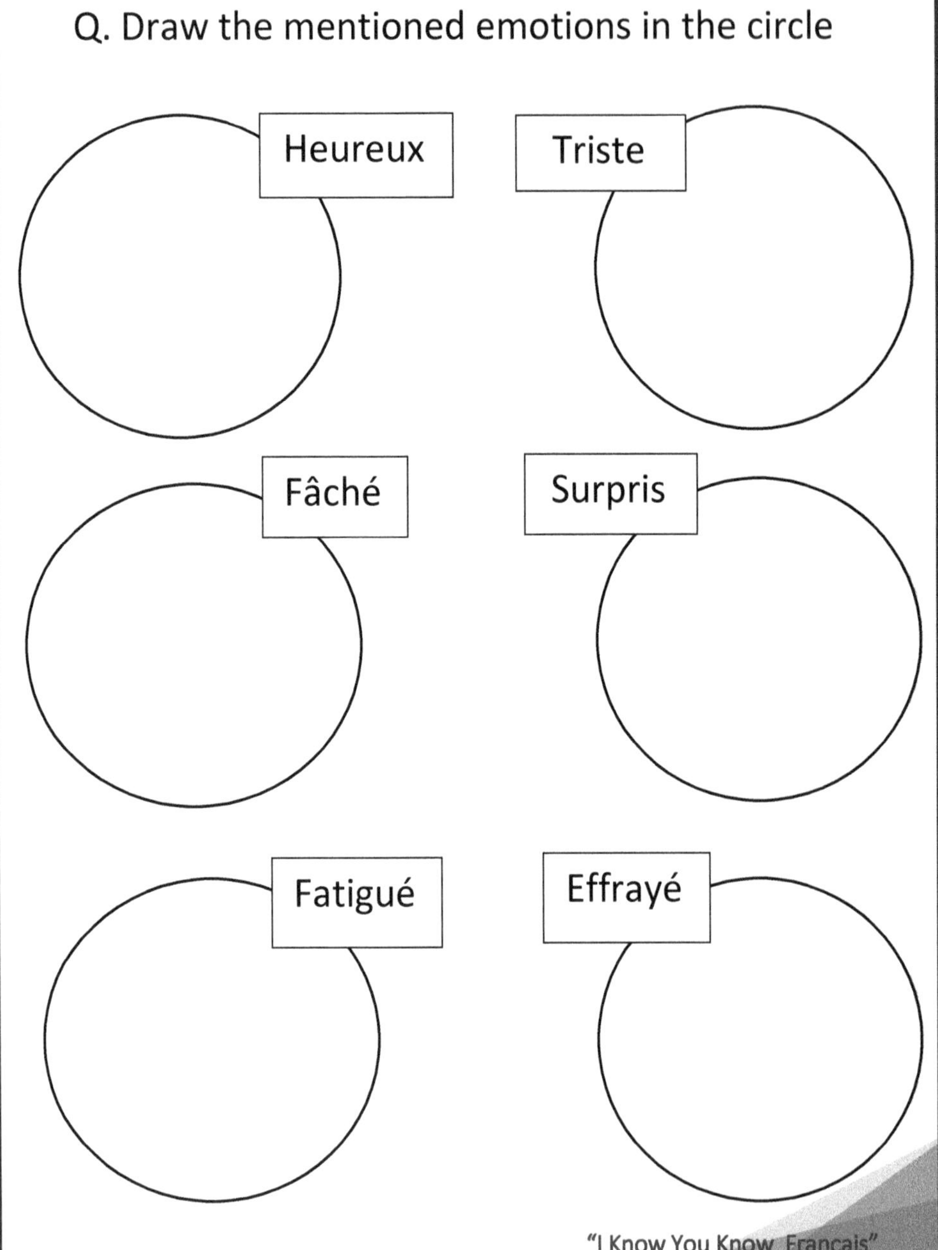

Les moyens de transport
(The means of Transport)

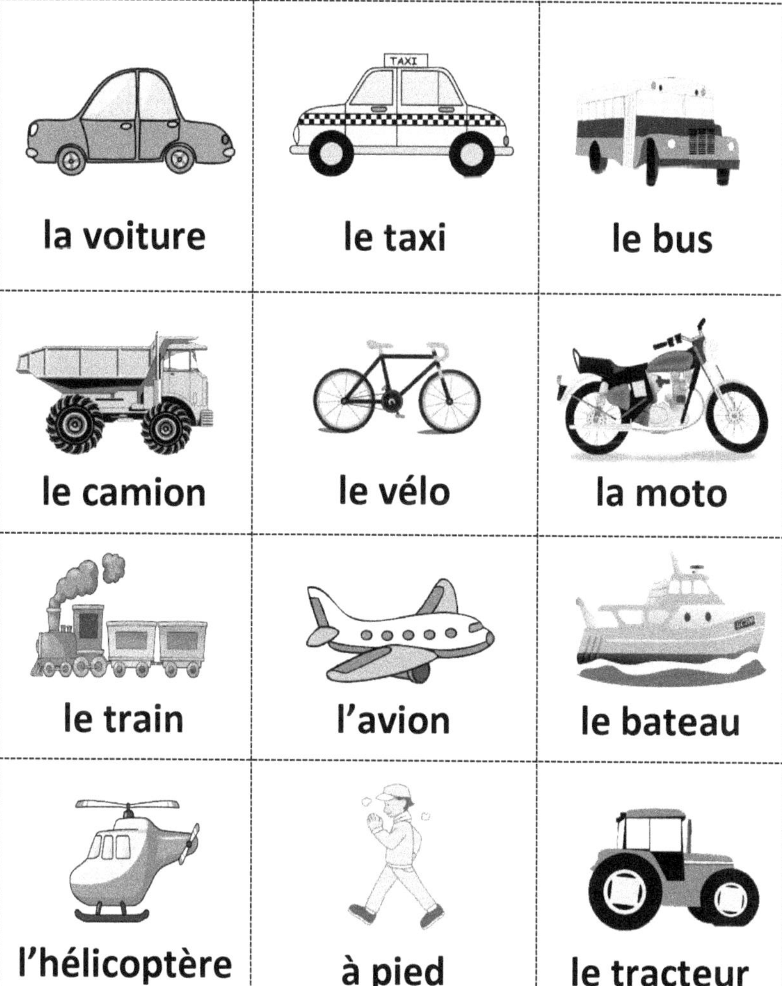

Activity

Q. Match the following

	l'avion
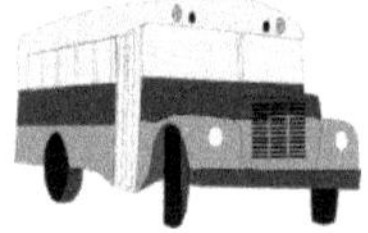	l'hélicoptère
	la voiture
	le bus
	le tracteur
	le bateau

Les nationalités
(Nationalities)

Pays (country)	Masculin	Féminin
L'Inde (India)	Indien	Indienne
La France (France)	Français	Française
L'Australie (Australia)	Australien	Australienne
La Belgique (Belgium)	Belge	Belge
L'Italie (Italy)	Italien	Italienne

L'Espagne (Spain)	Espagnol	Espagnole
La Russie (Russia)	Russe	Russe
La Suisse (Switzerland)	Suisse	Suisse
La Chine (China)	Chinois	Chinoise
Le Japon (Japan)	Japonais	Japonaise
Le Canada (Canada)	Canadien	Canadienne
L'Angleterre (England)	Anglais	Anglaise

L'Amérique (America)	Américain	Américaine
L'Afrique (Africa)	Africain	Africaine

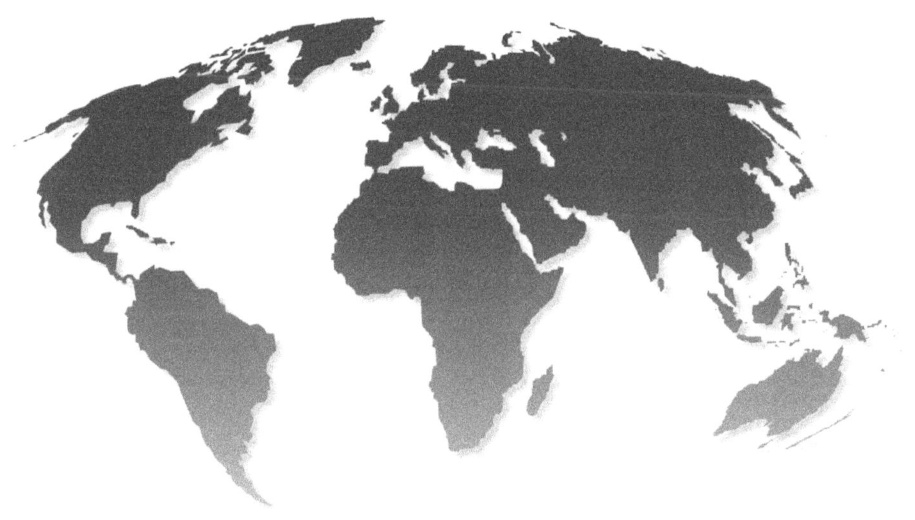

Activity

Q. Which flag represents which country?

Les adjectifs
(Adjectives)

	Masculin	Féminin
Tall	Grand	Grande
Short	Petit	Petite
Beautiful/ Handsome	Beau	Belle
Pretty	Joli	Jolie
Healthy	Sain	Saine
Kind	Gentil	Gentille
Good	Bon	Bonne
Young	Jeune	Jeune
Old	Vieux	Vieille

Grammaire

(Grammar)

Les Articles
(Articles)

What are articles?

In French, nouns are almost always preceded by an article. This indicates the gender of the noun (**masculine** or **feminine**) and its number (**singular** or **plural**).

There are **two** types of articles:

- ✓ Definite articles (**les articles définis**) Le, La, Les, L'
- ✓ Indefinite article (**les articles indéfinis**) Un, Une & Des.

How to say "**the**" - **Le, La, L', Les.**

In French there are different ways to say **THE**

It's different for masculine, feminine & plural.

For words starting with **vowel** (a,e,i,o,u) and some words starting with "**h**", **Le** or **La** is shortened to **L'** eg: **L'orange**, and **L'hôpital**.

One needs to also keep in mind that if the noun is **plural**, irrespective of the noun being **masculine** or **feminine** one has to use the term "**Les**" for the plural form.

Masculin Singulier	**Féminin Singulier**	**Devant les voyelles ou h muet Singulier**	**Mas/Fém/ voyelles et h mute Pluriel**
Le	La	L'	Les

- **Le** garçon → the boy
- **La** fille → the girl
- **L'**homme → the man
- **Les** garçons → the boys

How to say "**A**" – **Un , Une & Des**

In English it's easy. You say '**a**' for any word "a girl", "a boy", etc

In French, one needs to know whether the word is **masculine** or **feminine**, or **plural.**

There are **two** ways of saying '**A**': '**un**' & '**une**'

One needs to also keep in mind that if the noun is **plural**, irrespective of the noun being **masculine** or **feminine** one has to use the term "**Des**" for the plural form.

Masculin Singulier	**Féminin Singulier**	**Pluriel**
Un	**Une**	**Des**

- J'ai **un** frère - I have a brother.
- J'ai **une** sœur - I have a sister.
- J'ai **des** chaussettes - I have a pair of socks.

Verbs

Être and Avoir

The verbs **être** and **avoir** are two of the most important verbs in the French language. They can be used alone in the present tense or they can be used as auxiliary verbs to form the French compound tenses.

Avoir

Avoir means "**to have**", it is one of the most important verb. Not only does it means "**to have**" but **avoir** is also an important verb that creates the past tense, future tense and the past perfect tense.

Être

In almost every conversation you will need the French verb **être** Literally meaning "**to be**" conjugated with the various French subject pronouns, paired with adjectives, or used in numerous idiomatic expressions.

Avoir - “to have”

Singulier	Pluriel
• J’ai- I have	• Nous avons- We have
• Tu as- You have	• Vous avez- You have
• Il a- He has / It has	• Ils ont- They have (M)
• Elle a- She has / It has	• Elles ont- They have (F)

Être - “to be”

Singulier	Pluriel
• Je suis- I am	• Nous sommes- We are
• Tu es- You are	• Vous êtes- You are
• Il est- He is / It is	• Ils sont- They are (M)
• Elle est- She is / It is	• Elles sont- They are (F)

Activity

Q. Fill the blanks with the correct verbs

1) Nous (avoir) ___________ beaucoup de chance.

2) Vous (être) ________ libres ce weekend?

3) Ils (avoir) ____________ un chien qui s'appelle Max.

4) Tu (être) ___________ vraiment généreux.

5) Laura (être) ___________ très patiente et compréhensive.

6) Mon oncle (avoir) ____________ un appartement à Paris.

7) Tes grands – parents (être) __________en vacances à Milan.

8) Nous (être) ___________ en retard pour le match.

9) J'(avoir) ___________ de bonnes notes en anglais.

10) Je (être) _____________ américain.

11) Tu (être) _____________ allemande?

12) Tu (avoir) ____________ une jolie maison.

13) Il (être) ______________ jeune.

14) Elle (avoir) ____________ un frère.

15) Ils (être) ______________ contents.

16) Vous (avoir) ___________ une question?

17) Ils (avoir) _____________ peur.

18) Nous (être) ____________ ensemble.

19) Nous (avoir) ____________ terminé.

20) J'(avoir) _______________ une voiture rapide.

Common must know verbs

1. **Être (to be)**
   Je suis malade. (I'm sick)
2. **Avoir (to have)**
   J'ai un chien. (I have a dog)
3. **Aller (to go)**
   Je vais à l'école. (I go to school)
4. **Faire (to do)**
   Je fais mes devoirs.(I'm doing my homework)
5. **Aimer (to love / like)**
   J'aime la musique. (I love music)
6. **Manger (to eat)**
   Je mange une pomme. (I'm eating an apple)
7. **Boire (to drink)**
   Je bois du thé. (I'm drinking some tea)

8. **Dormir (to sleep)**
   Je dors à 21 h. (I sleep at 9pm)
9. **Laver (to wash)**
   Je lave la fenêtre. (I'm washing the window)
10. **Partir (to leave)**
    Je pars aujourd'hui. (I'm leaving today)
11. **Rester (to stay)**
    Je reste chez moi. (I'm staying home)
12. **Jouer (to play)**
    Je joue de la guitare. (I play the guitar)
13. **Acheter (to buy)**
    J'achète du pain. (I'm buying some bread)
14. **Vendre (to sell)**
    Je vends du pain. (I sell bread)
15. **Étudier (to study)**
    J'étudie avec un ami.
    (I'm studying with a friend)

16. **Travailler (to work)**

    Je travaille dur. (I work hard)

17. **lire (to read)**

    Je lis un livre. (I'm reading a book)

18. **Écrire (to write)**

    J'écris une lettre. (I'm writting a letter)

19. **Parler (to speak / talk)**

    Je parle au téléphone.
    (I'm taking on the phone)

20. **Marcher (to walk)**

    Je marche tous les jours. (I walk everyday)

21. **Commencer (to start)**

    Je commence la journée. (I start my day)

22. **Attendre (to wait)**

    J'attends le bus. (I wait for the bus)

23. **Compter (to count)**

    Je compte les billets. (I count the bills)

24. **Demander (to ask)**

    Je demande la permission.
    (I ask for permission)

Accents

There are five accents in French and each one is a guide to pronunciation.

1) L'accent aigu – (the acute) **é**

The accent changes the flat sound in **le** to a sharp sound like **préféré.**

2) L'accent grave – (the grave) **è à**

The accent changes the flat sound in **le** to a more open sound like **mère.**

3) L'accent circonflexe – (the circumflex) **ê â**

The accent often shows that an **'s'** is missing like **la forêt** and **la fête.**

4) La cédille – (the cedilla) **ç**

The accent softens the hard sound of **c** to a soft sound like **le garçon.**

5) Le tréma – (the trema) **ë**

The accent splits the two vowels into two sepreate sounds like **Noël.**

Dear Skill Builders,

Thank you for purchasing my book and I hope it has motivated you to pursue French further.

Wishing you all the very best.

Bonne Chance

Nilusha Judha

For further queries or feedback,

Contact on:

+91-8591253973

nilusha.ikykf@gmail.com

www.ingramcontent.com/pod-product-compliance
Ingram Content Group UK Ltd.
Pitfield, Milton Keynes, MK11 3LW, UK
UKHW021922190726
13853UKWH00002B/790